CHRISTMA

Savory Southern Christmas Favorites

HOLIDAY RECIPES & MORE

BARBOUR
PUBLISHING

© 2009 by Barbour Publishing, Inc.

Compiled by MariLee Parrish.

ISBN 978-1-60260-505-3

Scripture quotations marked NIV are taken from the HOLY BIBLE, NEW INTERNATIONAL VERSION®. NIV®. Copyright © 1973, 1978, 1984 by International Bible Society. Used by permission of Zondervan. All rights reserved.

Cover image left: Richard Eskite/Workbook Stock/Jupiter Images. Cover image right: Phillip Salaverry/Food Pix/Jupiter Images.

Published by Barbour Publishing, Inc., P.O. Box 719, Uhrichsville, Ohio 44683, www.barbourbooks.com.

Our mission is to publish and distribute inspirational products offering exceptional value and biblical encouragement to the masses.

Member of the
Evangelical Christian
Publishers Association

Printed in China.

Special thanks to Karen Parrish and Rebecca Dinsmore for sending me authentic recipes from their own kitchens in North Carolina. And thanks to Jeannie Hulse for sending me many Mississippi family recipes.

Merry Christmas Blessings,
Marilee Parrish

Contents

Drinks and Nogs

Suddenly a great company of the heavenly host appeared with the angel, praising God and saying, "Glory to God in the highest, and on earth peace to men on whom his favor rests."

LUKE 2:13–14 NIV

Festive Ice Cubes

Oranges
Pineapple
Strawberries

Maraschino cherries
Cranberry juice cocktail

Slice fruit into small pieces, leaving cherries whole. Place fruit in ice cube trays. Cover fruit pieces with cranberry juice cocktail. Freeze until solid. Drop in individual glasses or punch bowls.

Spiced Peach Cider

2 quarts peaches
2 cups water
1 cup sugar (or more to taste)

1 tablespoon whole cloves
½ teaspoon whole allspice
2 cinnamon sticks

Cut up fresh peaches and place in blender. Heat mixture on stove in large Dutch oven. Add water, sugar, and spices and bring to a boil. Reduce heat and simmer for 10 minutes. Strain mixture and discard spices. Return cider to Dutch oven. Cook over low heat until thoroughly heated. Serve warm.

Cranberry Punch

1 quart cranberry juice cocktail
1 (6 ounce) can frozen orange juice
   concentrate
2 (16 ounce) bottles ginger ale

Fresh cranberries
1 orange, sliced

Mix all liquids together. Garnish with fresh cranberries and oranges slices.
Serve cold.

Cherry Hot Cocoa

3 tablespoons unsweetened
   cocoa powder
¼ cup sugar
4 cups milk

1 teaspoon maraschino cherry
   juice (or more to taste)
Whipped cream
Maraschino cherries

Blend cocoa and sugar in small bowl. In medium saucepan, heat milk to scalding.
Mix about ⅓ cup hot milk into cocoa-sugar mixture then pour cocoa mixture
into hot milk in saucepan; stir until well blended. Stir in cherry juice. Pour into
mugs and top with whipped cream and a cherry.

Holiday Eggnog

2 large eggs
1½ cups sugar
½ teaspoon salt
2 quarts milk, divided

2 tablespoons vanilla
1 teaspoon ground nutmeg
2 cups heavy whipping cream

In 4-quart saucepan, beat eggs, sugar, and salt with wire whisk until blended. Gradually stir in 1 quart milk and cook over low heat. Stir constantly until mixture thickens, about 25 minutes. Do not boil. Pour mixture into large bowl; stir in vanilla, nutmeg, and remaining milk. Cover and refrigerate for at least 3 hours.

To serve: In small bowl, beat whipping cream with electric mixer until soft peaks form. Gently fold whipped cream into eggnog mixture with wire whisk. Pour eggnog into chilled 5-quart punch bowl and sprinkle with nutmeg.

Christmas Cheer Punch

1 (3 ounce) package raspberry gelatin
1 cup boiling water
1 (6 ounce) can frozen lemonade concentrate
3 cups cold water
1 quart cranberry juice
   cocktail, chilled

1 (12 ounce) bottle lemon
   lime soda, chilled
Festive Ice Cubes (recipe
   on pg. 8)

Dissolve gelatin in boiling water. Add lemonade. Add cold water and cranberry juice cocktail. Add soda and stir. Pour punch into chilled holiday punch bowl. Add several trays of Festive Ice Cubes.

Away in a manger, no crib for a bed,
the little Lord Jesus laid down His sweet head.
the stars in the sky looked down where He lay,
The little Lord Jesus asleep on the hay.

TRADITIONAL CAROL

Candy Cane Cooler

20 ounces frozen strawberries,
  unsweetened
1 (46 ounce) can pineapple juice

Lime sherbet
Peppermint candy canes

Place frozen strawberries in blender and puree. In large bowl, stir strawberry puree and pineapple juice. Pour into punch glasses. Top with spoonful of sherbet and hang candy canes on edge of cups.

Holiday Bubbly

1 gallon apple juice,
   chilled to almost slushy
1 gallon ginger ale,
   chilled to almost slushy
1 quart fresh or frozen
   strawberries

Mint leaves
Candy canes, various colors
   and flavors

Pour apple juice into large punch bowl. Slowly add ginger ale, pouring against side of bowl to maintain carbonation of ale. Add chilled strawberries one at a time. Float mint leaves on top, if desired. Serve in champagne flutes with candy canes hanging over edge of the glasses.

Montgomery Wassail

2¼ cups sugar
4 cups water
2 cinnamon sticks
8 whole allspice berries
1 tablespoon whole cloves

1 teaspoon ginger
4 cups orange juice
2 cups lemon juice
8 cups apple juice

In large saucepan, combine sugar and water. Boil for 5 minutes. Remove from heat. Add cinnamon sticks, allspice berries, cloves, and ginger. Cover and let stand in warm place for 1 hour. Strain liquid into large pot, discarding spices. Add juices and quickly bring to a boil. Remove from heat and serve.

Candy Cane Cocoa

4 cups milk
3 (1 ounce) squares semisweet
   chocolate, chopped
3 peppermint candy canes,
   crushed

1 cup whipped cream
4 small peppermint candy
   canes, crushed

In saucepan, heat milk until hot. Do not boil. Whisk in chocolate and the crushed peppermint until melted and smooth. Pour hot cocoa into 4 mugs and top with whipped cream. Serve with candy canes for stirring.

Crockpot Punch

3 cups orange juice
4 cups apple juice
6 cups cranberry juice cocktail
¾ cup maple syrup
2 teaspoons powdered sugar

1½ teaspoons cinnamon
1 teaspoon ground cloves
1 teaspoon nutmeg
Cinnamon sticks

Combine everything except cinnamon sticks in very large heavy pan. Bring to a boil and then let simmer for 3 minutes. Transfer to slow-cooker and keep warm over low heat. Not only is this a warm drink to have handy for company, but it will make your house smell like Christmas, too!

Jasper's Hot Chocolate

3 tablespoons unsweetened
   cocoa powder
¼ cup sugar
4 cups milk

¼ teaspoon vanilla
Whipped cream
Chocolate shavings

Blend cocoa and sugar in small bowl. In medium saucepan, heat milk to scalding. Mix about ⅓ cup hot milk into cocoa-sugar mixture. Pour cocoa mixture into hot milk in saucepan; stir until well blended. Stir in vanilla. Pour into mugs and top with whipped cream and chocolate shavings.

Breads and Biscuits

The shepherds returned, glorifying and praising
God for all the things they had heard and seen,
which were just as they had been told.

LUKE 2:20 NIV

Butter Pecan Bread

2¼ cups flour
2 teaspoons baking powder
½ teaspoon baking soda
½ teaspoon salt
¼ teaspoon cinnamon
¼ teaspoon nutmeg

1 cup light brown sugar
1 egg, beaten
1 cup buttermilk
2 tablespoons butter, melted
1 cup chopped pecans

Sift together flour, baking powder, baking soda, salt, and spices. Stir in brown sugar. Set aside. Combine egg, buttermilk, and butter. Add to flour mixture and blend well. Stir in chopped nuts. Turn batter into greased and floured 5×9-inch loaf pan. Bake at 350 degrees for 45 to 50 minutes or until wooden pick inserted in center comes out clean.

Pineapple Bread

1 (9 ounce) can crushed
   pineapple in syrup
2½ cups biscuit baking mix
⅓ cup sugar
4 tablespoons butter, softened

2 eggs
½ cup chopped walnuts
1 tablespoon sugar mixed
   with ¼ teaspoon
   cinnamon

Preheat oven to 350 degrees. Grease and flour 5×9-inch loaf pan. Drain pineapple well, reserving 3 tablespoons syrup. In mixing bowl, combine baking mix, sugar, butter, eggs, reserved syrup, and pineapple. Blend with electric mixer on low speed for 2 minutes. Stir in chopped walnuts. Pour batter into loaf pan and sprinkle with cinnamon-sugar mixture. Bake for 50 to 60 minutes or until wooden pick inserted in center comes out clean. Cool in pan for 10 minutes. Remove from pan and let cool on rack.

Vickie's Creamy Cranberry Bread

1 (8 ounce) package
  cream cheese, softened
1 cup butter
1½ cups sugar
1½ teaspoons vanilla

4 eggs
2¼ cups flour, divided
1½ teaspoons baking powder
½ teaspoon salt
2 cups fresh cranberries

Mix cream cheese, butter, sugar, and vanilla until smooth. Add eggs one at a time, mixing well after each one. Combine 2 cups flour, baking powder, and salt. Gradually add to butter mixture. Mix ¼ cup flour with cranberries and then fold into batter by hand. Batter will be thick. Spoon into 2 greased loaf pans. Bake at 350 degrees for 65 to 70 minutes. Cool in pan for 5 minutes and then cool on wire rack. Makes a great gift! Wrap in plastic wrap and then in aluminum foil. Tie with large ribbon and deliver to a special friend.

Special Occasion Banana Bread

⅓ cup chopped pecans
1 cup flour
¾ cup fine graham cracker crumbs
2 tablespoons ground baking chocolate
2 teaspoons baking powder
1 teaspoon baking soda

½ teaspoon salt
⅓ cup butter, softened
⅔ cup sugar
2 eggs
1 cup ripe bananas, mashed

Combine pecans with flour, graham cracker crumbs, chocolate, baking powder, baking soda, and salt. Mix well. Cream butter with sugar until fluffy. Beat in eggs, one at a time. Beat in mashed bananas until mixture is smooth. Stir in pecan mixture. Spoon into greased and floured 5×9-inch loaf pan. Bake at 350 degrees for 1 hour or until well done. Turn out onto wire rack to cool completely before slicing.

Blue Ridge Cinnamon Rolls

½ cup warm water
2 packages dry yeast
2 tablespoons sugar
1 (3½ ounce) package
   vanilla pudding mix

½ cup butter, melted
2 eggs
1 teaspoon salt
6 cups flour

Filling:
1 cup butter, softened
1 cup light brown sugar
4 teaspoons cinnamon

Mix water, yeast, and sugar until dissolved. Set aside. In large bowl, prepare pudding mix according to package directions. Add butter, eggs, and salt; blend well. Add yeast mixture and blend well. Gradually add flour. Transfer to lightly floured surface and knead dough until smooth. Place in greased bowl; cover and let rise in warm area until double in size. Punch down dough and let rise again until doubled. Roll out dough on floured surface. Spread 1 cup soft butter over surface. In small bowl, mix 1 cup brown sugar and 4 teaspoons cinnamon; sprinkle over the butter. Roll up tightly. Cut with sharp knife. Place cinnamon rolls on lightly greased cookie sheet 2 inches apart; lightly press each roll down. Cover and let rise to double again. Bake at 350 degrees for 15 to 20 minutes. Remove when rolls start to turn golden. Do not overbake. Frost warm rolls with cream cheese frosting. Makes about 20 large cinnamon rolls.

Apple Spice Bread

2⅔ cups flour
1½ teaspoons baking soda
1 teaspoon salt
2 teaspoons cinnamon
¼ teaspoon nutmeg
¼ teaspoon ground cloves
2 cups sugar
1 cup vegetable oil

4 eggs, beaten
2 teaspoons vanilla
4 cups chopped apples
1 cup raisins
1 cup chopped pecans
2 teaspoons sugar mixed
  with ¼ teaspoon cinnamon

Preheat oven to 325 degrees. Grease two 5×9-inch loaf pans and line bottoms with greased waxed paper. In large bowl, combine flour, baking soda, salt, and spices. Set aside. In mixing bowl, combine sugar and oil. Beat in eggs and vanilla. Stir in chopped apples, raisins, and pecans. Add dry ingredients and mix until well blended. Pour batter into pans, smoothing tops with spatula. Bake for 20 minutes. Sprinkle loaves with cinnamon-sugar mixture. Continue baking for 30 to 40 minutes or until wooden pick inserted in center comes out clean. Cool for 10 minutes; turn out onto wire rack. Slice and serve. This recipe freezes well.

Blueberry Biscuits for Christmas Morning

2¼ cups flour, divided
½ cup sugar
1 tablespoon baking powder
½ teaspoon fresh grated lemon
 peel
¾ teaspoon salt

Topping:
3 tablespoons butter, melted
2 tablespoons sugar

¼ teaspoon baking soda
⅓ cup shortening
1 egg, lightly beaten
¾ cup buttermilk
¾ cup frozen blueberries,
 do not thaw

¼ teaspoon cinnamon
Dash nutmeg

In large bowl, mix 2 cups flour with sugar, baking powder, lemon peel, salt, and baking soda. Cut in shortening until mixture is crumbly. Mix egg and buttermilk. Stir into flour mixture. Stir in frozen blueberries. Sprinkle remaining flour on countertop. Flour fingers and gently knead dough just until dough begins to hold together. Pat into ½-inch-thick rectangle. Cut with floured 2-inch round cutter. Place biscuits 2 inches apart on lightly greased baking sheet. Bake in center of preheated 400-degree oven for 12 to 15 minutes or until lightly browned. Combine topping ingredients and brush over warm biscuits.

*Go, tell it on the mountain,
over the hills and everywhere.
Go, tell it on the mountain
that Jesus Christ is born.*

JOHN W. WORK JR.

Pumpkin Pecan Bread

3 cups sugar
4 eggs
1 cup vegetable oil
1 (16 ounce) can pumpkin
3½ cups self-rising flour

1 teaspoon cinnamon
1 teaspoon nutmeg
½ teaspoon allspice
1 cup chopped pecans

In large bowl, combine sugar, eggs, and oil. With electric mixer, beat at medium speed until well blended. Stir in pumpkin. Combine flour and spices; gradually add to pumpkin mixture. Beat until blended then stir in pecans. Spoon mixture into 2 greased and floured 5×9-inch loaf pans. Bake at 300 degrees for 1 hour and 10 minutes or until wooden pick inserted in center comes out clean. Cool in pans for 10 minutes on wire racks. Remove from pans and let cool completely on wire racks.

Hush Puppies

2 cups cornmeal
1 cup flour
1 can kernel-style corn, drained
2 tablespoons minced onions
1 egg

2 tablespoons bacon drippings
1 teaspoon Cajun seasoning
2 tablespoons baking powder
¼ cup or more milk
Fat for frying

Heat at least 4 inches of fat in heavy pot or deep fryer. In medium bowl, mix all ingredients with just enough milk to make thick mixture. Wet hands and roll mixture into 1½-inch balls. Drop into deep fat and remove when brown. Drain on paper towels.

Buttermilk Biscuits

¼ cup shortening
2 cups self-rising flour, sifted

¼ teaspoon baking soda
1 cup buttermilk, minus
   1 tablespoon

Cut shortening into flour and baking soda until mixture resembles coarse crumbs. Add buttermilk and stir with fork. Turn dough onto lightly floured board and knead until smooth. Roll out dough about ½ inch thick and cut with floured 2-inch cutter. Place biscuits on lightly greased baking sheet and refrigerate until morning. Before serving, bake at 450 degrees for 10 to 12 minutes.

Mayonnaise Biscuits

1 cup whole milk
1 tablespoon sugar

2 tablespoons mayonnaise
2 cups self-rising flour

Mix all ingredients. Spoon dough into greased muffin tins. Bake at 375 degrees for 15 minutes or until golden brown.

Buttermilk Cornbread

3 cups buttermilk
1 egg
3 tablespoons baking powder

2 teaspoons salt
1 cup flour
2 cups cornmeal

Mix all ingredients. Place cast iron skillet in 350-degree oven to warm. Pour batter into preheated skillet and bake at 350 degrees until top is golden brown.

Country Cornbread Fritters

1½ cups hot water

2 cups self-rising cornmeal

2 eggs

¼ cup whole kernel corn

Mix all ingredients and fry in iron skillet with ½ cup hot cooking oil. Fry like pancakes, 3 or 4 minutes on each side. Fritters are done when they are golden brown.

Sides and Salads

"For God so loved the world that he gave his one and only Son, that whoever believes in him shall not perish but have eternal life."

JOHN 3:16 NIV

Red and Green Corn Casserole

2 cups milk, scalded
2 tablespoons butter, melted
2 eggs, beaten
2 cups frozen whole kernel corn,
  thawed
½ green bell pepper, finely
  chopped

½ red bell pepper, finely
  chopped
2 tablespoons finely chopped
  onion
1 teaspoon salt
Dash pepper

In large bowl, whisk milk, melted butter, and beaten eggs. Add corn, chopped pepper, onion, and seasonings. Pour into greased baking dish. Set dish in pan of hot water and bake at 350 degrees for 1 hour or until knife inserted in center comes out clean.

Candied Carrots

6 large carrots, peeled
12 small white onions, peeled
3 tablespoons butter
1 tablespoon sugar
1/3 cup light molasses

1/4 teaspoon salt
1/4 teaspoon ginger
1/4 teaspoon allspice
1 teaspoon chopped fresh mint

Using separate medium saucepans, cook carrots and onions, covered, in boiling salted water for 20 minutes or just until crisp-tender. Drain and set aside. Melt butter in large skillet; stir in sugar, molasses, salt, spices, and mint. Heat to boiling, stirring constantly. Add carrots and onions, stirring to coat well with syrup. Simmer, stirring frequently, for about 10 minutes.

Holiday Sweet Potatoes

6 large sweet potatoes
1 cup firmly packed light
    brown sugar, divided
½ cup butter, melted
⅓ cup half-and-half
2 large eggs

1 teaspoon vanilla
2 tablespoons flour
¼ cup cold butter,
    cut into pieces
2 cups gingersnaps,
    crumbled

Cover sweet potatoes in water and cook over medium heat for 30 minutes or until tender. Cool; peel and mash potatoes. In mixing bowl, combine mashed sweet potatoes, ½ cup brown sugar, melted butter, half-and-half, eggs, and vanilla. Beat on medium speed until smooth. Spoon into greased 9×13-inch baking dish. Combine ½ cup brown sugar and flour. Cut in cold butter with pastry blender until crumbly. Stir in crumbled gingersnaps. Sprinkle mixture over sweet potatoes. Bake uncovered at 350 degrees for 25 minutes or until topping is lightly browned.

Rebecca's Cornbread Dressing

1 medium onion, chopped
3 stalks celery, chopped
1 green pepper, chopped
2 tablespoons butter
1 (8 ounce) package dry
   cornbread stuffing
1 (8 ounce) package dry
   herb stuffing

½ cup buttered cracker
   crumbs
2 eggs
3½ cups chicken broth
Salt and pepper
 1½ teaspoons sage

Preheat oven to 350 degrees. Sauté onion, celery, and green pepper in butter until soft but not brown. In large mixing bowl, combine cooked vegetables, both dry stuffings, and cracker crumbs. Stir in eggs and chicken broth. Add salt and pepper to taste. Add sage. Mix well. Spoon into greased 9×13-inch glass baking dish. Bake for about 20 minutes or until set and lightly browned.

Creamy Mashed Potatoes

3 pounds potatoes,
    peeled and quartered
1½ sticks butter
6 ounces cream cheese, softened
1 cup shredded cheddar cheese, divided

1 small green pepper,
    finely chopped
6 green onions, finely chopped
½ cup grated Parmesan cheese
¼ cup milk
1 teaspoon salt

Cover potatoes with water and boil for 15 minutes or until tender; drain and mash. Add butter and cream cheese; beat with electric mixer at medium speed until smooth. Stir in ½ cup cheddar cheese, green pepper, onions, Parmesan cheese, milk, and salt. Spoon into lightly buttered 7×11-inch baking dish. Bake at 350 degrees for 30 to 40 minutes or until thoroughly heated. Sprinkle with remaining cheese; bake for 5 minutes or until cheese melts.

Festive Creamed Onions

2 pounds small white and
   purple onions, peeled
½ teaspoon salt
2 tablespoons butter
2 tablespoons flour

1½ cups whole milk
¼ teaspoon Cajun seasoning
¼ teaspoon paprika
Salt and pepper to taste
2 teaspoons chopped fresh
   parsley

Place onions in medium saucepan. Add ½ teaspoon salt and enough water to cover. Bring onions to a boil. Cover and cook for 20 minutes or until tender. Drain, reserving the cooking liquid. Set onions and cooking liquid aside. In same saucepan, melt butter and stir in flour. Gradually add milk. Cook, stirring constantly, until mixture thickens and begins to bubble. Stir in Cajun seasoning and paprika. Add salt and pepper. Add some of reserved liquid to thin the sauce if needed. Add onions to sauce and heat through. Garnish with fresh parsley.

Broccoli Pudding

1½ cups frozen chopped broccoli,
   cooked and drained
2 tablespoons butter
2 tablespoons finely minced onion
2 tablespoons flour
Dash pepper

⅛ teaspoon nutmeg
½ teaspoon salt
1½ cups half-and-half
1½ cups shredded sharp
   cheddar cheese
3 large eggs, beaten

Preheat oven to 350 degrees. Arrange broccoli in greased 2½-quart casserole. Heat butter in large skillet. Add onion and sauté until tender. Stir in flour until well blended. Cook, stirring, for 1 minute. Add pepper, nutmeg, salt, and half-and-half. Continue cooking over low heat until thickened. Stir in cheese and cook just until cheese is melted. Add about one-third of the hot mixture to beaten eggs. Add egg mixture to the hot cheese mixture and blend well. Pour over broccoli. Bake for 35 to 45 minutes or until knife inserted in the center of broccoli pudding comes out clean.

Stuffed Mushrooms

2 pounds medium-sized mushrooms
6 tablespoons butter
1 (8 ounce) package cream
  cheese, softened

½ cup crumbled blue cheese
3 tablespoons chopped
  green onion

Remove stems from mushrooms; chop stems to equal ½ cup. Set aside. Discard or freeze remaining stems. Cook 1 pound mushroom caps in 3 tablespoons butter over medium heat for 5 minutes. Drain and place on foil-lined cookie sheet. Repeat with remaining 1 pound mushroom caps and 3 tablespoons butter. In medium bowl, mix cream cheese and blue cheese until well blended. Stir in chopped stems and green onions. Fill mushroom caps. Broil until tops are golden brown.

Spinach Squares

3 (10 ounce) packages frozen
   chopped spinach
½ cup finely chopped onion
2 tablespoons butter
4 large eggs, beaten
2 cups milk

3 cups bread crumbs
1½ cups diced cooked ham
½ teaspoon seasoned salt
Hollandaise Sauce (recipe
   on p. 56)

Cook spinach according to package directions. Drain well. Over medium heat, cook onion in butter until tender. Combine beaten eggs with milk, bread crumbs, ham, cooked onion, spinach, and seasoned salt. Spread in 9-inch square baking dish. Bake at 350 degrees for 40 to 45 minutes or until set. Serve with warm Hollandaise Sauce.

Green Bean Supreme

1 pound frozen French-style
  green beans
1 small onion, halved and
  thinly sliced
1 teaspoon fresh parsley
3 tablespoons butter, divided
2 tablespoons flour
½ teaspoon fresh grated
  lemon peel

½ teaspoon salt
Dash pepper
½ cup milk
1 cup sour cream
½ cup shredded mild
  cheddar cheese
¼ cup dry bread crumbs

Cook frozen beans according to package directions; drain. Cook onion and parsley in 2 tablespoons butter until onion is tender. Stir in flour, lemon peel, salt, and pepper. Add milk and cook until thick and bubbly, stirring constantly. Add sour cream to green beans and stir in hot milk mixture. Heat until sauce begins to bubble. Spoon into 1½-quart casserole. Sprinkle cheese on top. Melt remaining 1 tablespoon butter and toss with bread crumbs. Sprinkle over cheese. Broil 1 to 2 minutes about 5 inches from broiler until cheese melts and crumbs brown.

Christmas Cabbage Dish

1 small head cabbage
1 small onion, chopped
8 slices bacon, diced
2 teaspoons vegetable oil
1 (10½ ounce) can cream
  of celery soup
¾ cup milk

½ cup mayonnaise
⅛ teaspoon pepper
2 cups fresh bread crumbs
3 tablespoons butter, melted
1 teaspoon chopped fresh
  parsley
1½ cups shredded sharp
  cheddar cheese

Lightly grease 3-quart baking dish. Cut cabbage into 4 wedges. Cut out core then cut each wedge crosswise into thin slices. Put cabbage in large saucepan and cover with water. Bring to a simmer. Cover and simmer for 10 minutes or until tender. Drain well and set aside. Sauté onion and diced bacon in oil until onion is tender. In large bowl, combine celery soup, milk, mayonnaise, pepper, and cooked onion and bacon. Add cabbage and stir to mix well.

In separate bowl, combine bread crumbs with melted butter and parsley. Toss to blend thoroughly. Sprinkle ⅓ cup bread crumbs over bottom of casserole. Top with cabbage mixture. Sprinkle cheese on top. Top with remaining bread crumbs. Bake uncovered at 375 degrees for 45 minutes.

Amazing Cauliflower

1 head cauliflower
1 large green pepper, chopped
1 large onion, chopped
1 teaspoon salt
3 tablespoons butter
3 tablespoons flour

1½ cups milk
1 cup shredded cheddar
   cheese, divided
½ cup butter-flavored cracker
   crumbs

Trim cauliflower into flowerets. Combine cauliflower with green pepper and onion in large saucepan. Cover with water and add salt. Bring to a boil. Cover and cook for about 10 minutes or until tender. Drain and set aside. In separate saucepan, melt butter over medium-low heat. Stir in flour until smooth and bubbly. Gradually add milk, stirring constantly. Continue cooking and stirring until thickened. Stir in ½ cup cheese. Pour sauce over cauliflower and stir gently. Transfer cauliflower mixture to lightly buttered 1½-quart baking dish. Top with cracker crumbs. Bake at 350 degrees for 30 minutes. Sprinkle with remaining cheese and bake 5 minutes longer.

Hollandaise Sauce

½ cup butter
2 egg yolks, beaten
2 tablespoons lemon juice

¼ teaspoon salt
Dash cayenne pepper

On low heat, melt butter in double boiler over simmering water. Whisk beaten egg yolks into butter, stirring constantly. Gradually add lemon juice. Continue to stir and cook until mixture is thickened and hot. Add salt and cayenne pepper before serving. If sauce is too thick, add 1 teaspoon hot water.

O come, all ye faithful,
joyful and triumphant,
O come ye, O come ye to Bethlehem!
Come and behold Him,
born the King of angels;
O come, let us adore Him…

JOHN F. WADE

Scalloped Corn Casserole

3 large eggs
1 cup half-and-half
1 tablespoon sugar
¼ teaspoon salt
⅛ teaspoon pepper

¼ cup finely chopped
    sweet onion
2 cups frozen cream-style
    corn, thawed
1 cup coarse cracker crumbs

In large bowl, whisk eggs and half-and-half. Add remaining ingredients and mix well. Pour into lightly buttered casserole. Bake at 350 degrees for 40 minutes or until almost set. Let stand greased for 5 minutes before serving.

Winter Squash Casserole

4 medium yellow squash, sliced
½ cup chopped onion
¼ cup butter, melted
2 hard-cooked eggs, chopped

½ cup shredded cheddar
cheese
½ cup butter-flavored cracker
crumbs

Cook sliced squash in small amount of boiling salted water for 10 minutes or until tender. Drain and set aside. Sauté onion in butter until tender. Combine drained squash, sautéed onion, butter, chopped eggs, and cheese in 1-quart casserole. Top with crumbs. Bake at 350 degrees for 20 minutes.

Spinach Bake

2 (10 ounce) packages frozen spinach
6 ounces cream cheese, softened
½ cup butter, melted, divided

1 cup seasoned bread crumbs
Dash paprika

Thaw spinach and press to remove excess water. Lightly grease baking dish and set aside. In large bowl, combine spinach, cream cheese, and ¼ cup melted butter. Spoon into prepared dish. Sprinkle with bread crumbs and paprika. Top with remaining ¼ cup butter. Bake at 350 degrees for 25 minutes.

Baked Succotash

2 (16 ounce) cans whole kernel corn
1 (16 ounce) can lima beans, drained
1 (12 ounce) can evaporated milk
1 cup shredded Monterey Jack cheese
2 large eggs, beaten
¼ cup sliced green onion

1 tablespoon chopped
  pimiento
⅛ teaspoon fresh ground
  black pepper
2 cups coarsely crumbled
  saltines, divided
2 tablespoons butter, melted

Drain corn, reserving liquid. Add water to corn liquid to equal ¾ cup. In large bowl, combine corn liquid, corn, lima beans, evaporated milk, cheese, eggs, green onion, pimiento, pepper, and 1½ cups cracker crumbs. Turn into greased 2½-quart casserole. Toss together remaining cracker crumbs and butter; sprinkle over casserole. Bake at 350 degrees for 55 minutes. Let stand for 5 minutes before serving.

Margie's Potato Salad

10 pounds red potatoes,
   cut into bite-sized pieces

6 to 8 hard-boiled eggs,
   chopped
Green olives, pitted and stuffed

Dressing:

Real mayonnaise (use enough to make
   salad a bit wet)
3 to 4 tablespoons Italian salad dressing
2 to 4 tablespoons sweet pickle relish
Celery salt to taste

Onion powder to taste
Garlic powder to taste
Black pepper to taste
1 tablespoon olive juice

Boil potatoes until tender but firm. Mix dressing ingredients and blend with potatoes and eggs. Make a day before to let all flavors blend. Before serving, slice green olives and use to decorate top of salad.

Maw Maw's Shrimp Salad

1 to 2 pounds medium shrimp
½ lemon
Crab boil seasoning
½ cup mayonnaise
3 tablespoons Italian salad dressing
2 to 3 hard-boiled eggs, chopped

2 tablespoons sweet pickle
  relish
½ cup finely chopped celery
2 tablespoons finely chopped
  green onion
Salt, pepper, and garlic
  powder to taste

Peel shrimp. Boil in water with salt, lemon, and 2 caps crab boil seasoning. Drain.
Mix shrimp with remaining ingredients.

Green Seven-Layer Salad

6 cups chopped lettuce
Salt and pepper to taste
6 hard-boiled eggs, sliced
2 cups frozen peas, thawed
1½ cups bacon, cooked crisp,
    drained, and crumbled

2 cups shredded cheddar
    cheese
1 cup mayonnaise
2 tablespoons sugar
¼ cup sliced green onion
Dash paprika

Place 3 cups lettuce in bottom of large bowl and sprinkle with salt and pepper. Layer egg slices over lettuce in bowl and sprinkle with more salt and pepper. Continue to layer vegetables in this order: peas, remaining lettuce, bacon, and cheese, along with light sprinklings of salt and pepper. Combine mayonnaise and sugar. Spread over top to edge of bowl, covering entire salad. Cover and refrigerate overnight. Toss before serving. Garnish with green onion and paprika.

Pearl's Cranberry Salad

1 (3 ounce) package cherry gelatin
1¾ cups hot water
1 cup fresh cranberries
½ orange with peel
⅓ cup sugar

½ cup crushed pineapple,
   drained
¼ cup pecans, chopped
1½ cups whipped topping

Dissolve gelatin in hot water. Set aside to chill until syrupy. Grind cranberries and orange. Add sugar, pineapple, and pecans. Add to gelatin. Chill until firmly set and spread whipped topping on top.

Creamy Cranberry Salad

1 (6 ounce) package cherry gelatin
2 cups hot water
1 (16 ounce) can whole
   cranberry sauce
1 (16 ounce) can jellied
   cranberry sauce

¼ cup lemon juice
8 ounces cream cheese, softened
2 cups whipped cream
½ cup chopped walnuts

Dissolve gelatin in hot water. Add cranberry sauces and lemon juice. Pour into lightly oiled cake pan. Chill until firm. Blend cream cheese, whipped cream, and walnuts. Spread on top of gelatin. Refrigerate for at least 3 hours before serving.

Strawberry Salad

2 (8 ounce) packages cream cheese
2 tablespoons mayonnaise
2 tablespoons sugar
2 (10 ounce) packages frozen
   strawberries, partially thawed
   and sweetened

2 cups miniature
   marshmallows
1 (12 ounce) can crushed
   pineapple, drained
3½ cups whipped cream
½ cup chopped walnuts

In large bowl, blend cream cheese, mayonnaise, and sugar. Add remaining ingredients. Pour into festive gelatin mold and freeze thoroughly. Remove salad from freezer 15 to 20 minutes before serving. Cut and serve.

Ambrosia Salad

1 can fruit cocktail, drained
½ cup mandarin oranges
½ cup pineapple tidbits
½ cup miniature marshmallows
½ cup sour cream

¼ cup maraschino cherries,
  halved
¼ cup red seedless grapes
Lettuce leaves

Drain all fruits. Combine all ingredients except lettuce in large bowl. Mix gently but thoroughly. Chill. Serve on lettuce leaves and garnish with additional festive fruits.

Orange Salad Delight

1 (3 ounce) package orange gelatin
1 cup hot water
1 cup cold water
3 tablespoons sugar
1½ cups mandarin oranges
2 medium bananas,
   sliced

1 cup green seedless grapes,
   halved
1 cup miniature marshmallows
½ cup chopped walnuts
Additional mandarin oranges
   and grapes for garnish

Dissolve gelatin in hot water; add cold water and sugar. Stir until sugar is dissolved.
Chill until partially set. Fold in mandarin oranges, banana slices, grape halves,
marshmallows, and chopped walnuts. Pour into gelatin mold and chill until firm.
Unmold onto bed of lettuce or greens and garnish with more mandarin oranges
and grapes.

Meats and Casseroles

Let the peace of Christ rule in your hearts,
since as members of one body you were
called to peace. And be thankful.

COLOSSIANS 3:15 NIV

Breakfast Casserole

10 slices bacon, diced
6 slices bread, lightly buttered
6 eggs, slightly beaten
2 cups milk

1 teaspoon salt
¼ teaspoon dry mustard
¼ teaspoon paprika

Cook bacon until browned and drain on paper towels. Cut bread into small pieces. In lightly buttered 2-quart casserole, layer bread pieces and bacon. In small bowl, whisk eggs, milk, salt, mustard, and paprika. Pour over bread and bacon. Bake at 350 degrees for 45 minutes or until puffy and knife inserted in center comes out clean.

Traditional Christmas Ham

1 (12 to 16 pound) Virginia ham
2 cups unsulfured molasses, divided
1 cup cider vinegar
3 whole cloves garlic
3 bay leaves

1 teaspoon peppercorns
3 or 4 whole cloves
Juice from large jar of
    sweet pickles
½ pound dark brown sugar

Begin preparing ham 2 days before serving. In large stockpot, cover ham with cold water. Add 1 cup molasses and cider vinegar. Allow to stand in cool place overnight. The next day, remove ham and drain liquid. Cover ham with fresh cold water and add remaining 1 cup molasses, garlic cloves, bay leaves, peppercorns, and whole cloves. Bring to a rolling boil over high heat and cover. Reduce heat slightly and boil for 30 minutes. Turn off heat but do not remove cover. Let stand in cool place overnight. Remove ham from water. Remove any rind. Using sharp knife, score ham diagonally. Push in whole cloves in even pattern to decorate and add flavor. Put ham in roaster, fattest side up. Mix pickle juice and brown sugar, adding just enough sugar until paste is formed. Spread ham with brown sugar paste. Bake at 350 degrees for about 60 minutes or until ham is nicely glazed.

Christmas Morning Casserole

2 tubes refrigerated crescent
  rolls
2 tablespoons butter
1 small onion, chopped
1 green pepper, chopped

½ cup fresh mushrooms
8 eggs
1 package sausage links
2 cups shredded cheddar cheese

Preheat oven according to crescent roll package directions. Press crescent rolls into 9×12 pan, pressing halfway up sides. Melt butter in saucepan. Sauté onion, green pepper, and mushrooms in butter. Set aside. In same saucepan, scramble eggs. Meanwhile, in separate saucepan, brown sausage links. Cool. Cut into small pieces. Layer eggs, mushrooms, onion, pepper, sausage, and cheese on top of crescent roll crust. Bake as directed on crescent roll package or until done.

Holiday Ham Steaks

4 to 6 ham steaks, about ½ inch thick
1¼ cups cranberry juice
½ cup light brown sugar
½ cup raisins

½ cup orange juice
2 tablespoons cornstarch
Dash ground cloves

Arrange ham steaks evenly in 9x13-inch baking dish. In saucepan, combine remaining ingredients. Cook and stir over medium heat until thick and bubbly. Pour over ham steaks. Bake uncovered at 350 degrees for 30 to 40 minutes. Great for Christmas morning!

Herbed Turkey with Maple Glaze

1 (12 to 14 pound) turkey
1 orange, unpeeled
1 Granny Smith apple, unpeeled
1 medium sweet onion
Salt and pepper
5 tablespoons butter, softened

2 teaspoons thyme
½ teaspoon rosemary
½ teaspoon marjoram
⅓ cup maple syrup
¼ cup brown sugar
¼ cup apple cider

Clean turkey inside and out. Sprinkle cavity with salt and pepper. Place turkey on rack in open roasting pan, breast side up. Cut orange, apple, and onion into large chunks and stuff into turkey cavity. Tie legs together with cooking twine. Sprinkle all over with salt and pepper. Combine butter with dried herbs in small bowl. Separate turkey skin from breast and push most of butter herb mixture evenly under each side. Rub turkey all over with remaining butter mixture. Wrap wing tips and drumstick ends with small pieces of foil. Loosely tent turkey with large piece of foil.

Roast for 2½ hours at 325 degrees. Remove and discard foil tent. Baste with maple mixture (maple syrup, brown sugar, and apple cider). Continue roasting, basting frequently, for 1 hour longer or until meat thermometer registers about 180 degrees when inserted in thickest part of turkey thigh.

Infant holy, Infant lowly,
for His bed a cattle stall;
oxen lowing, little knowing
Christ the Babe is Lord of all.

TRADITIONAL POLISH CAROL

Holiday Bayou Casserole

½ cup chopped green pepper
1 cup chopped celery
½ cup chopped onion
2 pounds fresh cooked shrimp
1 pound fresh cooked scallops
1 cup cooked rice
2 tablespoons butter

1 small jar pimientos,
   drained and chopped
¾ cup half-and-half
1 can cream of mushroom soup
1 cup mayonnaise
1 tablespoon Worcestershire
   sauce
Dash white pepper

Sauté green pepper, celery, and onion in butter. Toss all ingredients together and spoon into buttered baking dish. Cook uncovered at 375 degrees for 35 minutes or until heated through.

Carolina Tuna Casserole

4 tablespoons butter
3 tablespoons finely chopped onion
2 tablespoons finely chopped
  green pepper
2 tablespoons flour
¾ teaspoon seasoned salt
⅛ teaspoon pepper
1 cup milk
1 can cream of mushroom soup

8 ounces elbow macaroni,
  cooked and drained
1 (8 ounce) can tuna, drained
½ cup frozen peas, thawed
1 cup shredded cheddar
  cheese, divided
¼ cup butter-flavored cracker
  crumbs

Melt butter in large saucepan. Add chopped onion and green pepper and sauté over low heat until tender. Add flour, salt, and pepper. Cook, stirring constantly, until smooth and bubbly. Add milk and mushroom soup. Stir over low heat until smooth and thickened. Add cooked macaroni, tuna, peas, and ½ cup cheese to sauce mixture, stirring constantly. Pour mixture into buttered 2-quart casserole. Top with remaining cheese and cracker crumbs. Bake at 350 degrees for 30 to 40 minutes or until browned.

Turkey Noodle Casserole

½ cup butter
½ cup sliced fresh mushrooms
⅓ cup flour
2 cups chicken broth
1 cup milk
¼ cup chopped pimiento

2 teaspoons salt
½ teaspoon pepper
8 ounces egg noodles,
    cooked and drained
2 cups diced cooked turkey
⅓ cup grated Parmesan cheese

In large skillet, melt butter over low heat and sauté mushrooms. Blend in flour, stirring until smooth. Gradually add broth, milk, pimiento, salt, and pepper. Stir constantly until sauce is thickened. In buttered 2½ quart casserole, combine noodles, turkey, and sauce. Sprinkle Parmesan cheese top. Bake at 350 degrees for 25 minutes.

Sausage Casserole

1 pound mild pork sausage
1 large onion, chopped
½ cup diced carrots
¾ cup diced celery
1 (14½ ounce) can diced
    tomatoes, undrained
½ teaspoon thyme

¼ teaspoon oregano
1 teaspoon Cajun seasoning
1 teaspoon salt
⅛ teaspoon pepper
4 cups frozen baby lima
    beans, cooked and drained

In large skillet, brown sausage with chopped onion, carrots, and celery until vegetables are tender and sausage is no longer pink. Add tomatoes and seasonings and cook until hot and bubbly. Add lima beans and stir to combine. Transfer to lightly greased 2½-quart casserole. Cover and bake for 30 minutes at 350 degrees. Uncover and bake for 15 minutes longer.

Mainstay Macaroni Casserole

4 tablespoons butter
4 tablespoons flour
¼ teaspoon salt
⅛ teaspoon pepper
2 cups milk

¾ cup shredded sharp
   cheddar cheese
8 ounces elbow macaroni,
   cooked and drained

In medium saucepan, melt butter over medium-low heat. Stir flour into butter until smooth and bubbly. Stir in salt and pepper. Gradually add milk, stirring constantly. Continue to cook and stir until thickened. Add cheese and continue to cook and stir until melted. Alternate layers of macaroni and cheese sauce in 8×10-inch baking dish. Bake at 350 degrees for 20 minutes or until hot and bubbly.

Ham and Rice Casserole

2 cups cooked rice
2 cups diced cooked ham
1½ cups mixed vegetables,
   cooked and drained
1 (10½ ounce) can cream
   of mushroom soup

½ cup milk
½ teaspoon salt
¼ teaspoon pepper
1 cup butter-flavored
   cracker crumbs

In large bowl, combine cooked rice, ham, vegetables, mushroom soup, milk, salt, and pepper. Spoon mixture into buttered casserole and top evenly with cracker crumbs. Bake at 325 degrees for 30 minutes or until hot and bubbly.

Grits and Gravies

But the angel said to them, "Do not be afraid.
I bring you good news of great joy that will be for all the
people. Today in the town of David a Savior
has been born to you; he is Christ the Lord.
This will be a sign to you: You will find a baby
wrapped in cloths and lying in a manger."

LUKE 2:10–12 NIV

Fried Grits

¾ cup shredded sharp cheddar cheese
6 servings of grits, cooked as directs
2 eggs, slightly beaten

½ cup whole milk
Salt and pepper to taste
¼ cup butter

Stir cheese into warm grits until mostly melted. Place mixture in 9×12-inch casserole. Refrigerate overnight. In shallow dish combine eggs, milk, and seasonings. Cut grits into 3-inch strips and dip into egg batter. Fry in butter until golden. Serve hot.

Holiday Breakfast Grits

1 quart eggnog
5 tablespoons butter
1 cup uncooked grits

1 teaspoon salt
2 cups fresh blueberries

In large saucepan, warm eggnog and butter over low heat. Add grits and salt slowly while stirring. Keep stirring for about 25 minutes or until bubbly. Add blueberries and cook for 5 more minutes.

Grits and Redeye Gravy

¼ cup water
½ cup brewed coffee
½ cup ham drippings

6 servings of grits,
prepared as package directs

In iron skillet, add water and coffee to ham drippings. Cook over medium heat for 2 to 3 minutes. Spoon over hot cooked grits and serve.

Caramel Apple Grits

1 cup heavy cream
2 cups whole milk
1 teaspoon cinnamon
1 teaspoon salt
½ teaspoon vanilla
3 tablespoons brown sugar

¾ cup uncooked grits
3 Granny Smith apples, peeled
    and sliced just before serving
Butter and brown sugar
¼ cup caramel syrup

Lightly oil six 1-cup ramekins (small baking dishes) and set aside. In heavy saucepan, stir together cream, milk, cinnamon, salt, vanilla, and brown sugar. Bring to a boil and stir in grits. Cook over low heat, stirring frequently for 25 minutes or until thick and creamy. Spoon into ramekins and smooth tops with spoon. Cover with plastic wrap and refrigerate overnight. Before serving, sauté apples with butter and brown sugar until tender. Warm grits in microwave until heated through. Warm caramel syrup for 45 seconds. Unmold warm grits onto plate and top with syrup and apples.

Grits and Sausage

1 cup uncooked grits
4 cups water
½ cup margarine
1 tube prepared garlic
   cheese spread

3 eggs
½ cup milk
1 pound mild pork sausage,
   cooked and drained

In a large saucepan, cook grits in water for 5 minutes. Add margarine and garlic cheese spread. Stir until creamy. In separate bowl, beat eggs and milk. Add to grits. Add cooked sausage. Spoon into greased 9×13-inch casserole. Bake at 350 degrees for 45 minutes. Let stand for 5 minutes before serving.

Citrus Grits

1 cup water
½ cup orange juice
1 cup uncooked grits

⅛ teaspoon salt
2 tablespoons brown sugar

In medium saucepan, bring water and orange juice to a boil. Slowly stir in grits and salt. Reduce heat and simmer until thickened. Pour into serving dish and sprinkle with brown sugar. Let stand until sugar melts and serve.

Grandma's Sausage Gravy and Country Biscuits

Gravy:

1 pound seasoned pork sausage
2 tablespoons grease
2 tablespoons flour

2 cups milk
Salt and pepper to taste

Brown sausage and drain all but 2 tablespoons grease. Stir in flour and gradually add milk. Stir over medium heat until gravy thickens. Add salt and pepper. Serve over split Country Biscuits (recipe follows on page 96).

Country Biscuits:
2 cups flour
½ teaspoon salt
3 teaspoons baking powder

⅓ cup plus 2 tablespoons
    shortening, divided
1 cup milk

Sift dry ingredients into mixing bowl. Using pastry blender or fork, cut in ⅓ cup shortening until mixture resembles coarse crumbs. Add milk and mix until dough forms soft ball. Turn out on lightly floured surface; knead gently for 1 minute. Roll to ½ inch thick and cut with 2-inch round cutter. Melt 2 tablespoons shortening into baking pan. Place biscuits in pan, turning each side gets greased in melted shortening. Bake at 450 degrees until golden brown, approximately 15 minutes. Makes 12 to 15 biscuits.

Angels from the realms of glory,
wing your flight o'er all the earth;
ye who sang creation's story
now proclaim Messiah's birth.
Come and worship, come and worship,
worship Christ, the newborn King.

JAMES MONTGOMERY

Chicken Gravy and Biscuits

1 whole chicken, cut up
1 cup flour
Cooking oil

1 quart milk
Salt and pepper to taste

Coat chicken pieces with flour and fry until done in enough hot oil to cover. Remove chicken from heat and let cool enough to handle. Remove meat from bones. Discard skin, gristle, and bones. Add enough flour to pan drippings to make paste for gravy. Add milk slowly, stirring constantly. Add chicken and seasonings. Continue to cook and stir until gravy is thick and bubbly. Remove from heat. Serve over split hot biscuits.

Ham and Grits

3 cups water
½ teaspoon salt
Dash pepper
¾ cup uncooked grits
½ cup shredded mozzarella
   cheese

½ cup finely diced ham
2 tablespoons finely chopped
   green onion
2 eggs, separated
⅛ teaspoon hot sauce

In medium saucepan, bring water, salt, and pepper to a boil. Stir in grits. Cook, stirring often, for about 5 minutes or until thickened. Stir in cheese, ham, green onion, egg yolks, and hot sauce. In separate bowl, beat egg whites until stiff peaks form. Fold into grits. Pour mixture into buttered 1½-quart casserole and bake at 375 degrees for 30 minutes or until puffy and golden brown. Serve hot.

Creamy Chicken Gravy

3 tablespoons fried chicken drippings
3 tablespoons flour
2½ cups milk

½ cup heavy cream
Salt and pepper to taste

Leave 3 tablespoons drippings in skillet. Stir in flour until well blended; cook over medium heat for 2 to 3 minutes or until bubbly. Gradually add milk and cream. Boil until thick and smooth, stirring constantly. Add salt and pepper to taste.

Simple Turkey Gravy

¼ cup turkey pan drippings
¼ cup flour

Water
Salt and pepper to taste

Pour turkey pan drippings into 2-cup measuring cup and skim ¼ cup fat off. Add enough water to drippings to make 2 cups liquid. Place ¼ cup fat into saucepan and stir in flour. Pour 2 cups liquid into flour mixture. Cook, stirring constantly, until thick and bubbly. Add salt and pepper to taste.

Tomato Gravy

2 tablespoons olive oil
2 cloves garlic, minced
4 green onions, finely chopped
3 large ripe tomatoes,
    peeled and finely chopped

½ cup heavy cream
¼ teaspoon salt
¼ teaspoon ground red pepper
½ teaspoon dried thyme

In large skillet, heat oil over medium heat until hot. Add garlic and green onions. Cook for 5 minutes, stirring constantly. Add chopped tomatoes. Reduce heat and simmer for 3 minutes, stirring constantly. Stir in cream and seasonings. Continue to stir constantly and simmer until slightly thickened. Serve over chicken or pasta.

Pearl's Original Spaghetti Sauce

1 large onion, chopped
4 cloves garlic, cut in half
2 tablespoons oil
2 pounds lean ground beef
1 teaspoon salt
¼ teaspoon pepper
1 teaspoon sugar

1¼ teaspoons chili powder
2 large cans diced tomatoes
1 bay leaf
1 large can tomato sauce
2 teaspoons Italian seasoning
2 small cans tomato paste

In small saucepan, brown onion and garlic in oil over medium heat. In large saucepan, brown meat over high heat, stirring constantly. Add onion and garlic and remaining ingredients. Stir well and bring to a boil over medium heat. Reduce heat and simmer for 1 hour. Stir occasionally to avoid sticking. Remove bay leaf from sauce. Serve over your favorite pasta.

Old-Fashioned Giblet Gravy of the South

Giblets from 1 turkey
4 cups cold water
4 tablespoons butter
4 tablespoons flour
2 cups pan drippings

½ cup half-and-half
½ teaspoon salt
½ teaspoon pepper
2 hard-boiled eggs, chopped

Remove liver from giblets and refrigerate it. Place giblets in saucepan, cover with water, and bring to a boil. Reduce heat and simmer for 1 hour. Add liver and simmer for another 30 minutes. Drain in colander and allow to cool. Chop giblets and set aside. Melt butter in heavy saucepan and stir in flour. Cook and stir for about 3 minutes. Slowly stir in drippings and half-and-half. Continue cooking and stirring until thickened. Add salt and pepper. Stir in eggs and giblets. Serve warm.

Chocolate Gravy and Biscuits

Fresh baked biscuits
1 cup sugar
3 tablespoons flour

3 heaping tablespoons
    powdered chocolate milk mix
2 cups whole milk

Set biscuits aside. Combine all other ingredients in saucepan over medium heat and mix with whisk. Stir constantly until sauce takes on consistency of gravy, about 5 to 7 minutes. To serve, split biscuits and dot with butter. Spoon gravy over biscuits and serve immediately. Gravy will thicken on standing.

Sweets and Treats

"She will give birth to a son,
and you are to give him the name Jesus,
because he will save his people from their sins."

MATTHEW 1:21 NIV

Grandma Lucille's Pumpkin Pie

2 cups pumpkin
1 cup sugar
2 eggs, beaten
1 teaspoon cinnamon
¼ teaspoon ginger
¼ teaspoon nutmeg

1 teaspoon salt
1 (12 ounce) can
  evaporated milk
3 tablespoons butter, melted
1 (9 inch) unbaked pie shell
Whipped cream

Mix all ingredients together. Pour into unbaked pie shell. Bake 400 degrees for
10 minutes at and then reduce oven temperature to 350 degrees and bake for 65
minutes or until center is set. Serve with whipped cream.

Grammie's Peanut Butter Pie

⅓ cup peanut butter
¾ cup powdered sugar
1 large package vanilla pudding mix,
   prepared as package directs

2 cups whipped topping
1 (9 inch) baked pie shell

In small bowl, use pastry blender to combine peanut butter and powdered sugar; set aside. Line baked pie shell with one-third of peanut butter mixture. Top with prepared vanilla pudding. Cool. Top with whipped topping and sprinkle with remaining peanut butter mixture. Chill well.

Grandma Lucille's Strawberry Pie

1 quart stemmed and washed
   strawberries, crushing 1 cup
3 tablespoons flour

1 cup sugar
1 (9 inch) baked pie shell
Whipped cream

Cook 1 cup crushed berries, flour, and sugar over low heat until thick. Let mixture cool. Meanwhile, arrange some whole berries in bottom of pie shell. Alternate mixture and berries, ending with mixture. Top with whipped cream.

Fudge Pie

6 tablespoons flour
6 tablespoons cocoa
1½ cups sugar
1½ sticks butter, melted

3 eggs, slightly beaten
1 teaspoon vanilla
1 (9 inch) unbaked pie shell

In large bowl, sift flour, cocoa, and sugar. Add melted butter to eggs and stir. Add to dry ingredients. Stir in vanilla. Pour into pie shell and bake at 375 degrees for 30 minutes or until set.

Sweet Potato Pecan Pie

2 cups cooked, peeled sweet potatoes
½ cup unsalted butter, divided
½ cup heavy cream
½ cup packed light brown sugar
2 large eggs, slightly beaten
1 teaspoon vanilla
1 teaspoon cinnamon

1 teaspoon ginger
½ teaspoon nutmeg
⅛ teaspoon salt
2 tablespoons orange juice
½ cup dark corn syrup
1 cup chopped pecans
1 (9 inch) baked pie shell

In large bowl, mash sweet potatoes with ¼ cup butter. Let cool. Add heavy cream, brown sugar, eggs, vanilla, spices, salt, and orange juice. Beat until fluffy. Spoon into pie shell. Bake at 375 degrees for 20 minutes. Combine remaining ¼ cup butter with corn syrup and pecans. Sprinkle evenly over top of pie. Cover edge of crust with foil to prevent burning. Return pie to oven and bake 25 minutes longer or until wooden pick inserted in center comes out clean. Serve warm with whipped cream.

Grandma Lucille's Pecan Pie

1 cup pecans
1 (9 inch) unbaked pie shell
3 eggs
1 tablespoon butter, melted

1 cup light corn syrup
½ teaspoon vanilla
1 cup sugar
1 tablespoon flour

Arrange pecans in bottom of pie shell. Beat eggs and add butter, corn syrup, and vanilla. Stir until blended. Combine sugar and flour then blend with egg mixture. Pour slowly over pecans and let stand until pecans rise to top. Bake at 350 degrees for 45 minutes or until center is set.

Chocolate Pecan Pie

1 cup sugar
4 tablespoons butter, melted
3 eggs, slightly beaten
¾ cup light corn syrup
¼ teaspoon salt

2½ teaspoons vanilla
¾ cup pecans
½ cup semisweet chocolate
  chips
1 (9 inch) unbaked pie shell

Cream sugar and butter in mixing bowl. Add eggs, corn syrup, salt, and vanilla. Mix on low speed until blended. Spread pecans and chocolate chips in bottom of pie shell. Pour filling over pecans and chocolate chips. Bake at 375 degrees for 40 to 50 minutes or until set.

Pumpkin Cake

2 (16 ounce) packages pound
  cake mix
2 teaspoons pumpkin pie spice
2 teaspoons baking soda

Topping:
¾ cup brown sugar
¾ cup chopped nuts

⅔ cup water
1¾ cups canned pumpkin
  puree
4 eggs

½ cup flour
⅓ cup butter

Combine pound cake mixes, pie spice, and baking soda in large mixing bowl. Add water, pumpkin puree, and eggs. Beat on medium speed for 3 minutes. Set aside. Combine brown sugar, nuts, and flour in medium bowl. Cut in butter with pastry blender or fork until crumbly. Spread half of batter into greased and floured 9×13-inch baking pan. Sprinkle with half of topping. Carefully spread remaining batter; sprinkle with remaining topping. Bake at 325 degrees for 50 minutes or until wooden pick inserted in center comes out clean.

Gingered Pear Cake

4 medium-sized ripe pears,
   pureed
1 teaspoon vanilla
1 teaspoon lemon juice
1 teaspoon cinnamon
1 tablespoon ginger
1 cup whole milk
½ cup butter, softened
   (no substitutions)

5 eggs
1 cup brown sugar
½ cup unsweetened applesauce
3½ cups flour
1 tablespoon plus
   1½ teaspoons baking
   powder
Whipped topping

Mix the pureed pears, vanilla, lemon juice, cinnamon, and ginger in bowl. Set aside. Heat milk and butter in small saucepan until butter is melted. Meanwhile, beat eggs and brown sugar with electric mixer for 5 minutes or until pale and thick. Add milk and melted butter mixture while beating on low. Add pear mixture and applesauce. Sift flour and baking powder and add to mixture. Beat until just combined. Pour batter into greased and floured Bundt pan. Bake at 350 degrees for 55 minutes or until wooden pick inserted in center comes out clean. Serve warm with whipped topping.

Ding dong! Merrily on high
in heav'n the bells are ringing.
Ding dong! Verily the sky
is riv'n with angel singing.
Gloria, gloria,
hosanna in excelsis.

GEORGE R. WOODWARD

Simple Fruitcake

2½ cups flour
1 teaspoon baking soda
2 eggs, slightly beaten
1 (28 ounce) jar mincemeat
   with brandy and rum

1 (14 ounce) can sweetened
   condensed milk
2 cups mixed candied fruits
1 cup coarsely chopped nuts
Whipped topping

Combine flour and baking soda in large bowl. In separate bowl, combine remaining ingredients. Blend in dry ingredients. Pour batter into greased and floured 10-inch Bundt pan. Bake at 300 degrees for 1 hour and 45 minutes or until wooden pick comes out clean. Cool for 15 minutes. Turn out of pan. Garnish with whipped topping.

Pumpkin Pecan Pound Cake

3 cups flour
2 teaspoons baking powder
1 teaspoon baking soda
½ teaspoon salt
2 teaspoons cinnamon
½ teaspoon nutmeg
½ teaspoon ginger
¼ teaspoon allspice

1 cup butter (no substitutions)
1 cup sugar
¾ cup packed brown sugar
5 large eggs
1 (15 ounce) can pumpkin
   puree
1½ teaspoons vanilla
Maple Pecan Icing (recipe
   on page 125)

Combine flour, baking powder, baking soda, salt, and spices in large bowl. Set aside. In separate bowl, cream butter and sugars until light and fluffy. Beat in eggs, one at a time, beating well after each addition. Beat in pumpkin and vanilla. Slowly beat in dry ingredients. Continue beating on medium speed until smooth and well blended. Spoon into greased and floured 12-cup Bundt pan. Bake at 325 degrees for 55 minutes or until wooden pick comes out clean. Cool for 15 minutes in pan on wire rack. Then invert onto serving plate to cool completely. Drizzle with Maple Pecan Icing.

Quick Holiday Dump Cake

1 (16 ounce) can whole cranberry
   sauce
1 (21 ounce) can apple pie filling
1 box yellow cake mix

4 ounces butter
½ cup chopped pecans
Whipped topping

Dump cranberries into ungreased 9×13-inch baking pan. Dump apple pie filling into pan. Spread mixture evenly and sprinkle dry cake mix on top. Cut up butter and dot top of cake. Sprinkle pecans over cake batter. Bake at 325 degrees for 65 minutes or until wooden pick inserted in center comes out clean. Let cool. Serve with whipped topping.

Sweet Potato Cake

1 cup shortening
2 cups light brown sugar
3 eggs
1 cup baked and mashed sweet potatoes
3 cups cake flour

1 teaspoon cinnamon
3 teaspoons baking powder
1 teaspoon vanilla
½ cup milk
Coconut Icing
   (recipe on page 124)

In mixing bowl, cream shortening and brown sugar. Add eggs and sweet potatoes. Sift flour, cinnamon, and baking powder and add to mixture. Add vanilla and milk and mix well. Bake in 3 greased and floured cake pans at 350 degrees for 30 minutes.

Coconut Icing

1 (12 ounce) can evaporated milk
1 cup sugar
1 stick butter
3 egg yolks

1 teaspoon vanilla
1 cup flaked coconut
½ cup chopped nuts

Combine milk, sugar, butter, egg yolks, and vanilla in saucepan. Cook over medium heat for 10 to 12 minutes, stirring constantly until thick. Remove from heat. Add coconut and chopped nuts. Beat until cool. Spread between layers and on top of cake.

Maple Pecan Icing

4 tablespoons unsalted butter
3 tablespoons maple syrup
3 tablespoons heavy whipping cream

½ cup powdered sugar
2 tablespoons finely chopped
   pecans

In small saucepan, combine butter, maple syrup, and cream. Bring to a boil and boil for 1 minute. Remove from heat and whisk powdered sugar into hot mixture until smooth. Let cool for 15 minutes or until slightly thickened. Stir in pecans.

Easy Red Velvet Cake

1 box devil's food cake mix
1 (3.9 ounce) box chocolate
    pudding mix
1 teaspoon baking soda
1⅓ cups buttermilk
⅓ cup vegetable oil
3 large eggs

1 teaspoon vanilla
2 teaspoons white vinegar
1 (1 ounce) bottle red
    food coloring
Pecan Cream Cheese
    Frosting (recipe on page 127)

In mixing bowl, combine cake mix, pudding, baking soda, buttermilk, oil, eggs, vanilla, vinegar, and food coloring. Beat on low speed until well blended. Beat on high speed for 2 minutes. Pour batter into a greased and floured 10×13 baking pan. Bake at 350 degrees for 25 minutes. Cake is done when it springs back when lightly touched. Let cool on wire rack and frost.

Pecan Cream Cheese Frosting

4 ounces cream cheese, softened
1 teaspoon vanilla
1 (8 ounce) container whipped topping

1 cup powdered sugar
¼ cup finely chopped pecans

In mixing bowl, beat cream cheese, vanilla, and whipped topping until well blended. Slowly beat in powdered sugar until smooth and creamy. Add pecans and mix lightly.

Cinnamon Rice Pudding

1 cup salted water
½ cup uncooked rice
1 quart whole milk
¼ cup butter
3 eggs

½ cup sugar
½ teaspoon vanilla
½ cup raisins
1 teaspoon cinnamon

Boil water in Dutch oven. Pour rice into boiling water but do not stir. Cook for 7 minutes until rice is slightly done. Add milk and butter. Stir lightly and bring to a boil. Reduce heat and cover. Cook for 1 hour. Meanwhile, beat eggs, sugar, and vanilla. Pour over cooked rice. Stir slowly until rice starts to thicken. Add raisins and cinnamon. Serve warm. Store leftovers in refrigerator.

Easy Mini Cheesecakes

1 dozen vanilla wafers
2 (8 ounce) packages cream cheese
1 teaspoon vanilla

½ cup sugar
2 eggs

Line muffin pan with 12 foil liners. Place 1 vanilla wafer in each liner. In mixing bowl, combine cream cheese, vanilla, and sugar. Beat well. Add eggs and beat until well blended. Pour cream cheese mixture over wafers, filling each liner about three-quarters full. Bake at 325 degrees for 25 minutes. Garnish with fruit or chocolate.

Chocolate Sour Cream Sheet Cake

2 cups flour
1 teaspoon baking soda
½ cup sour cream
1 teaspoon salt
2 cups sugar
3 eggs, beaten

1 cup butter (no substitutions)
1 cup water
2 (1 ounce) squares
    unsweetened chocolate
Nutty Chocolate Icing
    (recipe on page 131)

In mixing bowl, combine flour, baking soda, sour cream, salt, sugar, and eggs. Mix well. Combine butter, water, and chocolate in saucepan. Bring to a boil. Add to egg mixture and mix well. Pour batter into greased sheet cake pan. Bake at 350 degrees for 25 minutes. Cool in pan.

Nutty Chocolate Icing

½ cup butter
⅓ cup milk
1 cup brown sugar
2 (1 ounce) squares milk chocolate

1 cup chopped peanuts
1 cup powdered sugar
1 teaspoon vanilla

Combine butter, milk, brown sugar, and milk chocolate in heavy saucepan. Bring to a boil. Do not stir. Boil for 3 minutes. Remove from heat. Immediately stir in peanuts, powdered sugar, and vanilla. Pour hot icing onto middle of cake and spread gently. Cool and cut into 2-inch squares.

Pumpkin Roll

3 eggs
1 cup sugar
⅔ cup canned pumpkin puree
1 teaspoon lemon juice
¾ cup flour
1 teaspoon baking powder

2 teaspoons cinnamon
1 teaspoon ginger
½ teaspoon nutmeg
½ teaspoon salt
Powdered sugar

Filling:

8 ounces cream cheese, softened
4 tablespoons butter, softened

1 cup powdered sugar
1 teaspoon vanilla

Combine eggs and sugar in large bowl. Beat well. Add pumpkin puree and lemon juice. Mix until blended. In separate bowl, combine flour, baking powder, spices, and salt. Add to egg mixture and mix well. Spread batter in 10×15-inch jelly-roll pan greased and lined with wax paper. Bake at 350 degrees for 15 minutes. Cool for 15 minutes. Place cake on clean tea towel sprinkled liberally with powdered sugar. Cool for 10 minutes. Starting with 10-inch side, roll up cake in towel. Set aside. In mixing bowl, beat cream cheese and butter. Stir in powdered sugar and vanilla and blend until smooth. Unroll cake, remove towel, and spread filling over cake evenly. Roll up cake and wrap in plastic wrap. Cover and chill for at least 1 hour. Slice and serve. Keep leftover slices refrigerated or frozen.

Pearl's Coconut Cake

1 box yellow cake mix
1 pint sour cream
1½ cups sugar

4 cups flaked coconut,
  divided
4 ounces whipped topping

Bake cake in layer pans according to package directions. Cool completely. Split each layer horizontally to make 4 layers. In large bowl, mix sour cream, sugar and 3 cups coconut. Set aside 1 cup frosting. Spread remaining frosting between the cake layers, stacking them to make 4-layer cake. Combine reserved sour cream mixture with whipped topping. Spread over sides and top of cake. Sprinkle remaining 1 cup coconut over entire cake. Cover and refrigerate for 3 days before cutting.

Grandma Woody's Miracle Whip Cake

2 teaspoons baking soda
1 cup warm water
1 cup sugar
1 teaspoon vanilla

1 cup Miracle Whip
4 heaping tablespoons cocoa
½ teaspoon salt
2 cups flour

Dissolve baking soda in warm water. Mix with ingredients. Pour into greased and floured 9×13-inch baking pan. Bake at 350 degrees for 45 minutes. Cool completely. Frost with your favorite icing.

Candies and Cookies

We have peace with God through
our Lord Jesus Christ.

ROMANS 5:1 NIV

Sour Cream Cutouts

2 eggs
1½ cups sugar
1 cup butter, softened
¾ cup sour cream
½ teaspoon salt

1 teaspoon baking soda
1 teaspoon baking powder
1 teaspoon vanilla
4 cups flour

Cream eggs, sugar, butter, and sour cream. Add remaining ingredients. Mix well and chill for at least 2 hours. Roll out on lightly floured surface and cut with your favorite holiday cookie cutters. Bake at 375 degrees for 10 minutes. Sprinkle with sugar or spices before baking, frost when cooled.

Grandma Woody's Oatmeal Cookies

1 cup shortening
1 cup sugar
1 cup brown sugar
2 eggs
1 teaspoon vanilla

1½ cups flour
1 teaspoon salt
1 teaspoon baking soda
3 cups quick oats

In mixing bowl, cream shortening, sugars, and vanilla. Add dry ingredients and mix well. Bake at 350 degrees for 15 minutes.

Cream Cheese Turtle Cookies

4 ounces cream cheese, softened
½ cup butter, softened
1 cup flour
20 pecan halves

1 (14 ounce) bag caramels,
  unwrapped
2 cups chocolate chips

Mix cream cheese and butter in medium bowl. Gradually add flour to form dough. Chill dough in refrigerator. Roll out and cut with floured 2-inch round cutter. Place cookies on ungreased cookie sheet and bake at 400 degrees for 12 minutes. Remove from oven and place unwrapped caramel on top of each cookie. Return cookies to oven and watch closely. Bake just until caramels are melted, about 5 to 6 minutes. Meanwhile, melt chocolate chips in double boiler or microwave. Slightly flatten caramels using buttered knife. Press pecan half into caramel on each cookie. Stir melted chocolate chips and spread 1 to 2 teaspoons over top of each cookie. Cool and serve.

Ginger Cookies

¾ cup shortening
1 cup brown sugar
¼ cup molasses
1 egg
2¼ cups flour
2 teaspoons baking soda

½ teaspoon salt
1 teaspoon ginger
1 teaspoon cinnamon
½ teaspoon cloves
Granulated sugar

Preheat oven to 350 degrees. Cream shortening, brown sugar, molasses, and egg until fluffy. Sift flour, baking soda, salt, and spices. Stir into molasses mixture. Form into small balls. Roll in sugar. Place 2 inches apart on greased cookie sheet and bake for 10 minutes. Do not overbake.

Lemonade Cookies

1 cup butter
1 cup sugar
2 eggs
3 cups flour
1 teaspoon baking soda

1 (6 ounce) can frozen
  lemonade concentrate,
  thawed and divided
2 teaspoons fresh grated
  lemon peel

In large mixing bowl, cream butter and sugar. Add eggs and beat until light and fluffy. Sift flour and baking soda; add to creamed mixture, alternating with ½ cup lemonade concentrate. Stir in lemon peel. Drop dough by teaspoonfuls, 2 inches apart, onto ungreased baking sheets. Bake at 400 degrees for 8 minutes or until lightly browned around edges. Brush hot cookies with remaining lemonade concentrate and sprinkle with granulated sugar. Remove cookies to racks. Makes 3 to 4 dozen cookies.

Old-Fashioned Sugar Cookies

½ cup butter
1 cup sugar
½ teaspoon vanilla or other flavoring
2 eggs

2 cups flour
2 teaspoons baking powder
¼ teaspoon salt
1 tablespoon milk
Granulated sugar

Preheat oven to 350 degrees. Cream butter and sugar; add vanilla and eggs. Mix thoroughly. Sift flour, baking powder, and salt and add to egg mixture. Add milk and mix well. Add enough additional flour to make cookie-dough consistency. Shape dough into ¾-inch balls. Place 2 inches apart on greased baking sheet. Flatten with bottom of glass that has been greased and dipped in granulated sugar. Bake for about 10 minutes.

Surprise Kisses

1 cup butter, softened
½ cup sugar
1½ teaspoons vanilla
1¾ cups flour

1 cup finely chopped pecans
1 bag chocolate kiss candies,
   unwrapped
Powdered sugar

In mixing bowl, cream butter, sugar, and vanilla. Blend in flour and pecans. Wrap 1 tablespoon dough around each chocolate kiss. Bake at 350 degrees for 15 minutes or until dough is set but not browned. Roll each cookie in powdered sugar while still warm.

God rest ye merry, gentlemen,
let nothing you dismay.
Remember Christ our Savior
was born on Christmas Day
to save us all from Satan's power
when we were gone astray.
O tidings of comfort and joy,
comfort and joy!
O tidings of comfort and joy!

TRADITIONAL CAROL

Pecan Snowballs

1 cup butter
1 tablespoon vanilla
¾ cup powdered sugar

2 cups flour
2 cups chopped pecans

In mixing bowl, cream butter and vanilla. Gradually add powdered sugar and flour. Add pecans and work into dough. Shape into quarter-sized balls. Place on greased baking sheets and bake at 300 degrees for 10 minutes. Increase oven temperature to 325 degrees and bake 5 to 10 minutes longer or until golden brown. Roll cookies in powdered sugar while still hot.

Raisin Pecan Tassies

1 cup butter, softened
6 ounces cream cheese, softened
2 cups flour
1 pound light brown sugar
3 eggs, beaten

3 tablespoons butter, melted
⅛ teaspoon salt
¼ teaspoon vanilla
½ cup golden raisins
½ cup chopped pecans

Combine butter and cream cheese with fork until smooth. Add flour gradually and work into smooth dough. Chill for several hours. Shape into quarter-sized balls and press into small muffin pans to make shells. In mixing bowl, slowly beat sugar and eggs. Mix in melted butter, salt, and vanilla. Put 5 raisins and ½ teaspoon pecans in each pastry shell. Pour filling over raisins and pecans to almost fill shells. Top with a few pecans. Bake at 350 degrees for 25 minutes or until set. Store in tightly covered container, between wax paper layers.

Milk Chocolate Oatmeal Cookies

5 cups quick oats
4 cups flour
1 teaspoon salt
2 teaspoons baking powder
2 teaspoons baking soda
2 cups butter, softened
2 cups sugar

2 cups brown sugar
4 eggs
2 teaspoons vanilla
4 cups chocolate chips
1 cup finely chopped peanuts
1 (8 ounce) milk chocolate bar,
    coarsely grated

Place quick oats in food processor and process until fine. In a large bowl, sift together flour, quick oats, salt, baking powder, and baking soda. In separate mixing bowl, cream butter and sugars. Add eggs and vanilla. Slowly add quick oats mixture and mix well. Add chocolate chips, grated chocolate bar, and nuts. Roll into balls and place 2 inches apart on ungreased cookie sheet. Bake at 350 degrees for 10 minutes.

Caramel Corn

3 quarts popped popcorn
3 cups dry roasted mixed
  nuts, unsalted
1 cup brown sugar
½ cup light corn syrup

½ cup butter (no substitutions)
½ teaspoon salt
½ teaspoon baking soda
1 teaspoon vanilla

In large roasting pan, combine popcorn and nuts. Place in oven at 250 degrees while preparing glaze. In medium saucepan, combine brown sugar, corn syrup, butter, and salt. Bring to a boil over medium heat, stirring constantly. Continue to boil for 4 minutes without stirring. Remove from heat. Stir in baking soda and vanilla and pour over warm popcorn and nuts. Toss to coat well. Bake at 250 degrees for 1 hour. Stir every 10 minutes. Cool and break apart. Store in airtight container.

Jake's Peppermint Fudge

3 cups semisweet chocolate chips
1 can sweetened condensed milk
1 teaspoon vanilla

½ teaspoon peppermint
    flavoring (*not* peppermint oil)
3 candy canes, crushed

In large microwave-safe bowl, combine chocolate chips and sweetened condensed milk. Microwave on high for 2 minutes. Add vanilla. Stir. Line 8-inch square pan with wax paper and pour in fudge. Sprinkle crushed candy canes on top. Carefully press candy canes into fudge so they will stick. Refrigerate.

Chocolate Truffles

⅔ cup heavy whipping cream
2 cups milk chocolate chips

2 teaspoons vanilla
Chopped nuts or cookie
crumbs

In medium saucepan, heat cream almost to a boil. Remove from heat and add chocolate chips. Whisk gently until chocolate is melted and mixture is smooth. Stir in vanilla and pour into bowl. Cover and refrigerate for 3 hours or until firm. When chocolate mixture is solid enough to work with, scoop into 1-inch balls and roll in finely chopped nuts or cookie crumbs. Place truffles on waxed paper; cover loosely and chill overnight. Store in tightly covered container.

Pralines

1 cup half-and-half
4 cups sugar, divided
1½ teaspoons vanilla

2½ cups coarsely
chopped pecans
⅛ teaspoon salt

In large saucepan, boil half-and-half with 3 cups sugar until small amount forms soft ball when dropped into very cold water. Meanwhile, melt remaining 1 cup sugar in heavy skillet, stirring constantly over medium-low heat until sugar reaches brown caramel stage. Add caramel sugar to half-and-half mixture, stirring with long wooden spoon. Test again for soft-ball stage. Remove from heat and cool to lukewarm. Add vanilla, pecans, and salt and beat until creamy and stiff. Drop onto buttered wax paper. Let cool. Remove from wax paper and store in tightly covered container.

Creamy Pralines

½ cup evaporated milk
1¼ cups sugar
¾ cup brown sugar

4 tablespoons butter, frozen
1 tablespoon vanilla
1½ cups pecans

In large saucepan, boil milk and sugars until small amount forms soft ball when dropped into very cold water. Remove from heat. Add frozen butter, vanilla, and pecans. Beat until creamy and stiff. Drop onto buttered wax paper. Let cool. Remove from wax paper and store in tightly covered container.

Popcorn Mix

10 cups popped popcorn
1 cup raisins
2 cups graham cracker cereal
1½ cups miniature marshmallows
¼ cup butter, melted

¼ cup light brown sugar
2 teaspoons cinnamon
½ teaspoon nutmeg
¼ teaspoon ginger

Combine popcorn, raisins, cereal, and marshmallows in large roasting pan. Stir until well blended. Combine remaining ingredients in small bowl and stir into popcorn mixture. Bake at 250 degrees for 20 minutes. Stir halfway through baking time. Let cool. Store in tightly covered container.

Sweet and Southern Snack Mix

2 quarts popped popcorn
½ cup pecans
½ cup candy corn

24 caramels
1 tablespoon water
1 tablespoon sugar

In large bowl, combine popcorn, pecans, and candy corn. Melt caramels, water, and sugar in top of double boiler over boiling water. Stir to blend. Pour melted caramel over popcorn mixture. Toss to mix thoroughly. Shape into ½ cup mounds and place in paper cupcake liners to serve.

Cinnamon-Sugar Pecans

1 egg white
1 tablespoon water
1 cup sugar
¾ teaspoon salt

1 teaspoon cinnamon
¼ teaspoon ground cloves
¼ teaspoon ginger
1 pound pecan halves

Beat egg white and water until frothy but not stiff. Stir in sugar, salt, and spices. Add pecans and stir until completely coated. Spread pecans on large baking sheet and bake at 200 degrees for 45 minutes, stirring every 15 minutes. Remove from oven when dry and toasted. Store in airtight container.

Berry Patch Caramel

2⅔ cups brown sugar
1 cup light corn syrup
1 (14 ounce) can sweetened condensed milk

1 cup butter
1 teaspoon vanilla

Bring all ingredients to a boil, stirring constantly until temperature reaches 245 degrees or firm-ball stage. Remove from heat and add vanilla. Pour into greased 9-inch square pan. Cool. Cut into squares. Wrap in cellophane candy wrappers.

Index